SARAH K. HOWLEY

I AM

THE SON REVEALS THE FATHER

AN 8-SESSION
STUDY OF JOHN

I Am:

An 8-Session
Study of John

The Son Reveals the Father

By

Sarah K. Howley

I Am: An 8-session Bible Study of John

Copyright © 2021 Sarah K. Howley

Flaming Dove Press
an imprint of
InspiritEncourage LLC
1602 Belle View Blvd #5081
Alexandria, VA 22307
www.inspiritencourage.com

ISBN   978-1-7369071-3-9 (e-pub)

ISBN   978-1-7369071-5-3 (paperback)

Cover and interior design: Sarah K. Howley

Printed in the United States of America

Library of Congress Control Number: 2021914004

Table of Contents

Welcome to this Study
of the 'I AM' statements from
the Gospel of John

The heart of this study comes from Psalm 9:10, 'Those who know your name trust in you, for you, Lord, have never forsaken those who seek you.' Study of the names that Jesus gave for himself then surely must increase our trust in him and lead us to knowing him more intimately. The depth of our knowledge of Jesus should not rest merely at *knowing of* him but should develop the relationship that we have with him. This leads to the thought that knowing a name is not enough to develop trust, the name must have an underlying sense of the being. As John 17: 3 says, 'Now this is eternal life: that they know you, the only true God, and Jesus Christ, whom you have sent,' therefore in knowing Father and Son, we will find eternal life. This eternal life, according to the Hebrew word, is the unique quality of God's life at work in us, as a present possession[1]. And so began this study to *know* Father and Son through some of the names Jesus gave, encouraging that life to work in us.

As Hebrews 1:3 tells us that Jesus is 'the exact representation of his [the Father's] being', we have the opportunity to *view the Father through the lens of the Son in these identifying phrases.* This study looks at Jesus' 'I AM' passages from John and passages in the Old Testament which echo the heart of the message of these statements and reveal the way in which the Old Testament has reflected the name.

---

[1] https://biblehub.com/greek/166.htm, 23 February 2021.

Each session opens with warm-up introductory questions, goes on to a reading from John and questions related to the passage. Then the study goes to the linked Old Testament passage and questions. Each study session ends with considerations for personal application. Additional tips and suggestions on approaching the study for individuals and groups follow.

Suggestions for Study

This study is designed for individual or small group study, with 8 sessions. It is designed to encourage thought and discussion of the scripture with no one 'right answer', but rather encourage individuals and groups seeking God to have discussions. For 'You will seek me and find me when you seek me with all your heart,' as Jeremiah 29:13 says.

General Guidelines for Individual Study

1. Open each session with prayer. Ask God to speak through his Word.

2. Respond to the **Introduction** questions to focus on the theme of the session and what Jesus says in the main reading.

3. Read the passage more than once. Using different translations can offer expanded viewpoints on the meaning of the original text. This study uses the New International Version as the basis of questions and quotes. However, any version may be used to provide insight and assist in revealing meaning.

4. This study is designed to offer a starting point for discovery of what God has to say to you through his Word. Because the study looks at how Jesus reveals the Father in these passages, there are *observation* and *interpretation* questions about the readings in John and then about the links in the Old Testament, as well as comparisons between the passages. These are followed by *application* questions for personal and group discussion. Writing your responses will provide clarity and focus your thoughts on the verses.

5. Use a Bible dictionary or other reference books to look up any unfamiliar words, places, or names.

General Guidelines for Group Study

1. Come to sessions prepared. Some groups will choose to read and respond ahead of time then gather and discuss together; others will gather to read and discuss together. Before beginning, agree how you would like to proceed so all are prepared.

2. Be an active participant in the group by sharing your thoughts and responses to the questions. Groups often have members who are of varied maturity in Christ and each perspective should be valued.

3. Listen to each other. Consider the amount of time that is available for all to share and be careful not to dominate the conversation.

4. Be open. As there are no 'right' or 'wrong' answers, be open to considering alternate viewpoints and agree to disagree.

5. Maintain confidentiality of the group. For participants to be willing to share and grow, the trust level in the group must be high. Do not share outside the group unless permission is given to do so.

6. Expect God to meet you in the study. His Word is living and active (Heb. 4:12) and he is present when we gather in his name (Matt. 18:20).

Study Introduction

The English language uses 'My name is...' as an introduction, however most Latin languages use the equivalent of 'I am...' as an introduction. It seems like more than a name when we use this phrase. It is more closely related to identity; we expect an adjective to come after the phrase 'I am'. God himself uses the phrase *I Am* as an introduction and many of the Psalms proclaim that God is... good, faithful, our refuge, our help. God is described in many ways by the writers of the Bible. So, before we look at how Jesus described himself, consider these introductory questions.

How would you finish the statement about yourself: I am ...

Who is Jesus to you? He is ...

Session 1
I AM the Bread of Life, John 6:25-59

Introduction

Other than food, what does bread in general mean or symbolize to you?

What phrases do you use with bread in them? Does your culture have phrases about bread or rice or the main staple of your country? Also share some food idioms.

Bread is a common food staple for many cultures around the world. We know we can survive a long time with just bread and water. There is also bread for every person: croissant, toast, bagel, gluten-free, and that is just breakfast. Every meal has its accompanying bread, rice, or similar starch around the world. Jesus didn't choose bread randomly. He chose something that we can identify with as a foundation of our physical health and tied it to our spiritual health. Not having our Daily Bread is like living without sustenance of a meal.

Read John 6:25-59.

Questions

Who is the audience of this discourse?

What does 'Bread of Life' say about the character of Jesus?

What other gifts are offered to believers with this bread in verses 35-51?

What must the audience do to receive this Bread of Life?

At this point in time, the Last Supper has not been instituted. What does 'eats my flesh and drinks my blood' (verse 54) mean?

Old Testament Links

Both the audience and Jesus talk of the manna in the wilderness. Jesus compares the Bread that he offers to the manna of the wilderness, but the manna did not give the same life. He made the statement as a clear indication of importance of daily communion with and dependence upon God. Read Exodus 16, which describes the situation of God's people and the gift of manna and consider it in relation to the Bread of Life.

Manna sounds like Hebrew for 'what is it?' How could this relate to Jesus?

Consider the following questions for each of the passages:

	Manna Exodus 16	Bread of Life John 6:25-59
What is the origin of it?		
What need does it meet?		
How does it impact life? How does it impact death?		
Who was/is it for?		
How long does it last?		
Who pays the cost? to whom?		
What was the recipient's attitude?		

Deuteronomy 8:3 references manna as well. How does Jesus echo what it says?

Exodus 25:23-30 and Leviticus 24:5-9 describe the bread of the Presence in the tabernacle set up in the wilderness. Read these passages and discuss how this may be similar or dissimilar to the Bread of Life.

Application

What does the statement 'I am the Bread of Life' say about Jesus? About Father? Do you embrace it fully?

Have you received the 'Bread of Life'? What has receiving it produced in your life?

Do you eat his flesh and drink his blood, as you defined above? If not, what would you do differently?

How is Jesus the better manna?

Session 2
I AM the Light of the World - John 8:12-20, 12:35-36

Introduction

What comes to mind when you hear the word 'light'?

How do you respond to being in dark places?

Jesus is called not only the Light of the World, but also the 'bright Morning Star' (Rev. 22:16). Repetition of ideas underscores importance in the Bible. Light dispels the darkness of the unknown, of insecurity and ushers in hope, warmth, and clarity of vision. Jesus is the Light of the World who unveils the unknown and guides us through it.

Read John 8:12-20; 12:35-36.

Questions

Who is Jesus talking to in these two passages? How do they respond to him?

By replacing the word *I* with *Light* in verse 15, we have 'Light passes judgment on no one.' Discuss the truthfulness of this statement.

What are the benefits to those who follow the light according to the passage?

What kind of darkness do people walk in? How do they not walk in darkness with the Light?

Old Testament Links

Light related to God was not a new concept in Jesus' time. The New Testament use of light more specifically associates light to God; and it brings to life associated characteristics from the Old Testament. Jesus' embodiment of the character of God shines forth in the Old Testament verses that speak of light.

Note what light describes in the following verses: Exodus 13:21-22, Daniel 2:22, Isaiah 9:1-7.

In Psalm 27:1, Psalm 43:3, Psalm 119:105, 130 light is not mentioned alone. What accompanies light in the verses?

Exodus 37:17-24 and Leviticus 24:1-4 describe the lampstand in the tabernacle. What do the placement of it and its construction tell you of it as well?

Genesis 1:3 is reflected in John's opening verses, 1:1-10. How does this elaborate on the meaning of the 'Light of the World'?

How does the Old Testament present light in comparison to the way it is presented in the New Testament?

Application

In Matthew 5:14, Jesus states, 'You are the light of the world.' Given the discussion during this session, what does being light mean for believers?

In the tabernacle, the lampstand was to be tended daily and filled with clear olive oil. What does this say about Jesus? What does this say about our worship?

John's mission in writing the Gospel, according to John 20:31, is that 'you may believe that Jesus is the Messiah, the Son of God and that by believing you may have life in his name.' Discuss why light may have been included to support this mission.

Session 3
I AM the Door (Gate) – John 10:1-10

Introduction

How are doors and gates a comfort? In what situations might they not be comforting? What other emotions does a door bring to mind?

When expecting visitors and greeting them at the door, what do you do? Does that change based on your familiarity with the visitors?

A door marks a gateway from one area to another. Jesus as the gateway to God and the gateway to peace and refuge is a powerful representation of what he is and does for us. There is a marked point of our coming and going which defines the area where beyond that door, storms may rage, cars may race, fires and arms may be set in the midst of the neighborhood, but the house is a refuge. Just as Jesus is our refuge.

Read John 10:1-10.

Questions

Jesus uses the metaphor of a sheep pen in these verses. Take a moment to discuss what each of the aspects in the metaphor may stand for: pen, area outside the pen, gatekeeper, thief/robber/stranger, sheep.

What is the difference between being called the gate and the gatekeeper?

In these verses, what do the sheep do? And not do?

Old Testament Links

It is interesting to note that the pen is only used for a specified period of time, overnight for example. There is a time when the Shepherd leads us back out. We cannot stay forever in this idyllic place at least not in this world, but we are welcome regularly to gather and find restoration behind him, the door that he is.

Psalm 118:19-24 includes one of the rare mentions of a gate or door in the Old Testament. What does the psalmist demonstrate is the importance of the door?

The entrance to the courtyard of the tabernacle was also a type of gate. Found in Exodus 27:9-19, compare the courtyard to the sheep pen of John 10.

Application

Consider the qualities of doors/gates and the emotions discussed in the first question of the session. Which of these do you associate with Jesus Christ?

Which of Jesus' qualities do you demonstrate when meeting with people? Are there any that you would like to incorporate?

Are your own tendencies more of a gatekeeper, gate, or sheep? Does it change at times according to situations? Describe how you act that way and which characteristics you may prefer to take on.

Session 4
I AM the Good Shepherd - John 10:11-21

Introduction

What are the characteristics of a good leader?

What kind of follower are you? What role do you play in a group?

The shepherd is a grand example of a leader, while the sheep are animals which are dull of mind. However, the shepherd, as leader, develops a relationship with the sheep, he feeds them, provides for them, cares for them. They know his voice. Sheep trust the One they know, whose voice they recognize. We too are called to that same blind trust of the One.

Read John 10:11-21.

Questions

Jesus contrasts the hired hand to the good shepherd in this passage. Summarize these differences.

Jesus mentions the Father in three verses (15, 17, 18) of this short passage. How do the words know, love, and authority connect to us (the sheep), in the relationship between Father and Son according to these verses?

What is the response of those who hear these words?

Old Testament Links

The shepherd as leader of Israel was not a new idea for Jesus' audience. They were likely familiar with the comparison, but perhaps were not happy with the rebuke of the hired hand. However, the rebuke is a good reminder to assess our actions and thoughts, to check our pride and ensure our hearts are open to love – love God and love others.

Read Chapter 34 of Ezekiel, typically titled 'The Lord will be Israel's Shepherd'. For further references to the shepherd in the Old Testament and time permitting, consider also reading Isaiah 40:9-14, Jeremiah 23:1-8, Micah 5:2-7, and/or Psalm 23.

	Old Testament Passages	The Good Shepherd John 10:11-21
Who are the sheep?		
Who had care of the flock before? Who does this represent?		
What will happen to those shepherds?		
What have they done wrong?		
What have they left undone?		
Who now has care of the flock?		
What does this shepherd do?		
What blessings do the sheep receive under the shepherd?		

Exodus 27:1-8 outline the requirements for the construction of the altar at the tent of meeting in the tabernacle. Exodus 29:38-43 and Leviticus 16:15-16 outline the sacrifice requirements. Discuss why Jesus is often identified as the altar of the tabernacle.

Application

What does it mean to have the Good Shepherd as your leader? Do you consider God as the Good Shepherd your leader? What may be challenging about accepting this?

When you review the list of blessings for the flock from the Old Testament Links table, are there any that you are lacking? Discuss why this might be.

Session 5
I AM the Resurrection and the Life – John 11:1-44

Introduction

Share about any dreams or relationships that have died away or need a breath of fresh air. How have you felt about this 'dead' status of these dreams and relationships?

What makes a life worth living?

Dreams may die away or become impossible, like having a child at 90 years old was impossible for Sarah (Gen. 18:12). Yet Sarah's dream had not died, she laughed because she understood that it was not naturally possible; but she likely still desired it. She acted on it even though it was impossible and conceived. God knows our dreams and knows how to breathe life into them even when they seem dead.

Read John 11:1-44.

Questions

Who was the audience in verse 25, when Jesus says, 'I am the resurrection and the life'? Why would this be significant?

What hints does Jesus give through the passage about his intention to resurrect Lazarus?

What are the main ideas of the short prayer before Jesus calls Lazarus from the grave (verses 41-42)?

What do Mary and Martha say to Jesus about his power? How does Jesus respond?

What characteristics of the Christian walk do Martha and Mary show in this passage?

Old Testament Links

Four days dead yet the power of God has raised Lazarus. He was a friend to Jesus and Jesus wept over the pain and loss. He is your friend too and weeps over the losses you have experienced. He raised the dead to life and can still.

Read Ezekiel 37:1-14, the passage titled 'The Valley of Dry Bones' and discuss the following questions in relation to the John 11 passage:

What is the condition of the bodies in the valley? And that of Lazarus?

List some similarities and differences in the responses of Ezekiel to God and the sisters to Jesus.

When do the bones come alive? When does Lazarus come alive?

What do these passages say of the power of God?

The Bible tells of many people who have been given new life through his power. For example, we have Noah who is saved from the flood and Daniel kept from the lions. Consider others and discuss how they were delivered from harm and/or difficult situations.

Application

The bones in the valley not only animated physically, but the breath from four winds was also put in them. In John, Lazarus needed help to remove the graveclothes. How could these parallel what happens in our own lives in resurrecting life, dreams, and relationships?

Share praise stories of your own deliverance from harm and difficult situations.

Share and pray about the resurrections that God has put on your heart. Consider dreams and relationships as well as characteristics of Christian living, like hope or joy.

Session 6
I AM the Way and the Truth and the Life – John 14:1-15

Introduction

Most of us have either gotten lost heading to a new place or we have been given unclear directions to assist us in arriving somewhere unfamiliar. Tell how this made you feel and what you did about it. What condition were you in when you arrived?

Discuss the relationship between belief, trust, and truth.

The path, the actual fact, the breath – these synonyms all fall short of describing this phrase of Jesus. He is the bridge that carries us to God himself. Jesus clears the old and makes a way for us to reach the Father. Jesus reveals the reality that we may see distortedly, he fills us with everlasting life.

Read John 14:1-15.

Questions

Jesus says he is the way. Where does the way lead? What does following the way require?

What truth does Jesus embody?

How is life imparted according to the passage?

What are the results of belief according to Jesus in this passage?

What does the passage teach about prayer?

Old Testament Links

God has desired an intimate relationship with each of us since the creation of Adam in the Garden of Eden. He sought such a relationship with the Israelites and seeks one still today with you. Sending Jesus fulfilled the need for atonement for sin but does not turn our hearts automatically to God. He leaves the choice to us, to be his child or not. The Old Testament also tells of his desire for us to be his children.

Read the following passages and consider how they present the way, truth, and life in the Old Testament. Deuteronomy 30:19-20, Psalm 1:1-3, Psalm 25:1-15, Psalm 56:12-13, Psalm 139:23-24, Isaiah 35:1-10, Isaiah 65:16, Daniel 12:2-3.

Read Exodus 26:31-35 and Matthew 27:51-53. What do these passages indicate about Jesus' statement, 'I am the way, the truth, and the life'?

Application

If you had been present for the events of Matthew 27:51-53, how would you have responded? If it happened again today, what would you do?

The passage discusses the results of belief, as asked in the questions above. Share these as you have seen them in your own life.

How has the truth changed you, or sanctified you, as you have known him?

What can believers do to know, or better know, the way, truth, and life?

Session 7
I AM the True Vine – John 15:1-17

Introduction

What do you find motivates you or gives you energy to get things done?

What makes your home special to you?

These verses of the True Vine challenge us to consider our home in the vineyard, as branches. We are called to consider the source of our being and our fruit-bearing. Making our dwelling the vine is more than reflecting his character, it is becoming his character and seeking him as that something special of our being. All that flows in the vine shall flow through to the branches, nourishing and growing the branch.

Read John 15:1-17.

Questions

How does Jesus describe God in this passage?

How are followers described?

What is the duty of the branches?

How do followers bear fruit? Who is the fruit for?

What does abiding in him mean or look like?

How is love connected to fruit bearing?

Old Testament Links

The New Testament is based upon the demonstration of love that Jesus is and represents. The Old Testament also shows this same love of God for his people. He cared as much in the Old Testament for his people as in the time of and since Jesus' coming. He made clothing for Adam and Eve in Genesis, he delivered his people from slavery through Moses, and he set a king over them as they asked. God has tended his vines, caring for his people all through the Bible.

Read Isaiah 5:1-7 and 27:2-6.

Who is the vine?

What has the vinedresser done for the vines?

How has the vine responded?

Read Psalm 80:8-19.

What kind of scene do verses 8-11 evoke?

Why are the vineyard walls broken down and the vines cut and burned?

What hope is seen in these verses?

Discuss how Jesus can be the true vine when Israel was the vine in the Old Testament.

Application

What fruit have you borne and who has benefited from it?

What kind of home does Jesus have in you? How has he made it special?

What has the vinedresser cleaned, or pruned, off your branch so it may bear more fruit?

Session 8
I AM He – John 4, 6, 8, 13, 18

Introduction

How do you introduce yourself compared to how others introduce you?

If you could ask Jesus to explain anything, what would you ask him?

Jesus announces who he is throughout the gospels. He does not make it a mystery that he has come to fulfill the Word of God and *not* to abolish the law. Just as we often ask people to repeat their name so we can get it right and respect their identity, Jesus also repeats his name for us to know exactly who he is and understand his identity. He invites us with each introduction to come closer and know him more intimately.

Read John 4:5-26, 6:16-21, 8:21-24, 8:48-59, 13:18-20, 18:3-8.

Questions

In each passage, note who the audience is and their response to Jesus saying, 'I am' or 'I am he'. What does the response tell you of their understanding of Jesus?

What does Jesus declare of himself each time he makes the statement? Is there a characteristic that is emphasized in the encounter?

Old Testament Links

Jesus does not keep his identity hidden. In the Old Testament, God reveals who he is in numerous encounters. Recognizing God is left to the individual; to believe or to seek to understand is an individual choice. The invitation to each person is personally made and can only be personally answered, *I Am* has called you.

Exodus 3:9-15. What are the three names that God gives for himself in verses 14 and 15?

What do these names say of his nature?

God says Moses should tell the Israelites, '*I Am* has sent me to you'. How does Jesus also carry this message to the Israelites?

Application

The John 4 and 6 passages are revelations to small groups or just a few people. How has Jesus revealed himself to you personally?

Share occasions when God has revealed himself to you while in a group or in church. Discuss the similarities and differences between the personal revelations and the group ones.

Study Conclusion

The study of these names Jesus gave himself and the linked Old Testament verses offers an opportunity to better understand the underlying sense of his character through his names. John's Gospel chooses these statements to reveal Jesus' identity so that '...you may believe that Jesus is the Messiah, the Son of God, and that by believing you may have life in his name,' (John 20:31). 'Life in his name' has a unique quality and comes through an ever-deepening relationship with him, including through studying his Word.

How have Jesus' statements in these 8 sessions revealed the Father to be?

What is your image of the Father? Has it changed over the course of the study? If so, describe the change.

Do you believe that Jesus is the Messiah, the Son of God and have you received life in his name? If so, describe the qualities of that life.

If this is the first time that you have answered yes to the call of *I Am*, please reach out to a local church or the author to share of your choice and find support for your new life.

To continue understanding how Jesus reveals the Father, *Heart* shows you how in the lessons of Jesus. Find it on Amazon by scanning the QR code today.

Acknowledgments

Thank you to my Lord and Savior Jesus Christ for His redeeming work and guidance in writing this study.

Thank you to my family and friends, and especially my husband, who have supported and encouraged me in all the writing I do.

Thank you, readers, for choosing this resource to know God more deeply. If you liked this book, please check out my site, https://www.inspiritencourage.com, for more Christian encouragement. I love to hear from readers, so please reach out.

Please Review this Book!

Was this book helpful? Did you get something from it? Please help others find this resource by visiting Amazon or Goodreads and leaving a review of this book. Every review makes this book more visible to others. Follow the QR code to write a review now.

https://www.amazon.com/review/create-review?asin=B097MPTH6D

About the Author

Sarah K. Howley is an author of Christian nonfiction for women. Her first book is titled *Alive Again: Find Healing in Forgiveness*. Sarah is a certified Christian counselor and holds a master's degree in education but prefers the authority of her Bible over those pieces of paper. She was born in Houston, Texas and has lived on four continents. When not writing at inspiritencourage.com, you can find her eating dark chocolate, sipping espresso, reading, or planning her next trip.

You can find Sarah on Instagram or Facebook @inspiritencourage.

To receive notices of Sarah's upcoming books, sign up at https://www.inspiritencourage.com/subscribe

Other Books by Sarah K. Howley

Alive Again

Alive Again: Find Healing in Forgiveness
Alive Again Bible Study: Find Healing in Forgiveness
Alive Again Forgiveness Prayer Journal

The Son Reveals the Father

Heart: A 12-Session Study of Luke
Word: An 11-Session Study of Matthew
King: An 8-Session Study of Mark

Made in the USA
Las Vegas, NV
27 March 2024